Devouring The Sun

Brad R. Weekley

A Dream Darkly Lit

In dream I walked a morbid hall,
Drawn to heed some hastening call.
Upon a carpet of dark magenta,
Thick lines reveled in the dementia,
Of the artist that willed them to perversion
Of curves entwined to be as one.

Censors wrought of silver suspended,
By hooks or so were bended,
Adorned the space between velvet tapestries
That alluded to forbidden mysteries;
But only a moments glance had they,
For a touch sinister commanded me this way.

I came to gaze upon a mirror black,
For all the features it did lack,
Mine eyes transfixed and would deter not.
This was the obsession I had sought.
My hand stirred by a will not my own,
To caress this void of obsidian tone.

The instant flesh met devouring echo,
I transported to a most foreboding portico,
Looming atop a marble staircase waiting,
Coy in its insidious intentions flirting.
My dread intensified each step I did creep,
Seduced to tread this menacing steep.

Pillars of corrupted Corinthian loomed,
Supporting chiseled demons doomed,
To bear the harsh crown till vicious legacy
Be purged from recollection and prophecy.
At length I reached the height of my desire,
Compelled to ascend beyond the evergreen spire.

There the source of my enthrallment embodied
In the allure of feminine vice levied
To capture all passion remaining leaving this;
Indifference for but only a serpent's kiss.
For all my insight I stood petrified,
For this Gorgon's stare held me though it lied.

Through force of will mine eyes found diversion
From eyes that reeked of rancid perversion.
Though seductress lay upon lecherous charms,
Enough to make men lay down their arms,
And submit to defiled hands machinations,
Yet I waylay mine eyes from the core of fascinations.

Her hips swayed as daisies in delight,
Masking the pendulum's swinging fright.
Her obscene gown twirling about in a charade
Put on for this her midnight masquerade.
"My love," she said, "My one, came to me for solace
Let my heart warm you in its furnace."

My throat burned at this 'till "Liar!" I cried,
"Thou would have it that love had died
To be held in mine heart nevermore!
Thou art lust and nothing more!
Beautiful abomination tempt me not!
You are not the loveliness I have sought!"

"What foul beast doth feign its name be love,
To propel by discharge of a moments fancy above?
Better to give my heart some other whore,
One whose skill in treachery be not of lore.
Wretched beast if thou doth insist,
I shall give thee eye and keep my fist."

"Can you see the squall in my eye?
Look quick to find thine doom and die-
For thine image is reflected back
Upon thine empty spheres of black.
Thee gave me the means of thine own destruction
In all that I endured in thine dysfunction!"

In memory, sweet memory, in memory I hear laughter
Which shall be heard again in the bitter hereafter.
Forsaking frigid whores lonely comforts,
Leave them to the patronage of perverts,
For I shall walk through this night alone
'Till dawn does find me when love has shown.

A Shades Transition

An inspiration sought
By illuminating death
Casts new shadows
Dancing in the eyes
Of those that can embrace
A new darkness

Borrowed Breaths

I love you
Wait
Scratch that-
It's not enough
Let me start over
I'll try to do better
This time
This sensation's too much to condense
But I'll try
For you

I borrow the breath of roses
Drunk on imitation of you
The wind often wishes
Its tempest could tease
your hair
For a moment
To have a memory worth keeping
What I'm trying to say is

I love you
Wait
Scratch that-
It's not enough
Let me start over
I'll try to do better
This time
This sensation's too much to condense
But I'll try
For you

Silkworms labor in vain
To compare your lips to their efforts
Angels in choir often conspire
To steal your voice
For a sound that swells
The seas as they swoon
With my heart
What I'm trying to say is

I love you
Wait
Scratch that-
It's not enough
Let me start over
I'll try to do better
This time
This sensation's too much to condense
But I'll try
For you

Wait
Scratch that
It's not enough
It's not enough
It's not enough
It's not enough
Wait

I want to tell you
But the words escape me
Wait here forever
With me

Carnival

The things we embrace in the light
Seldom reflect the attractions
Of the night's carnival.
The maddening rush of forbidden desires
Seduces the mind's eye
More than any trick of light.

Caution

Caution
Grim life zones
In the box underneath
Open valve
Apply flame
Release the spirits
Within

Corrupted Crusaders

Our will shall impose on the masses throughout.
We will wipe out the evils of this world,
But the haunting red spot won't wash out.
For we abandoned the lofty ideals we held,
To find the demons in others we seek to quell,
Find sanctuary in our own hearts and dwell.

Deadly Nightshade

She paints her face with smeared light
In praise of the glamor of vice.
Her eyes retract the lines of ambition
While her lips embrace its lust.

She permits the longing of limbs
To consume a moments attention,
As drawn breath recedes
To grasp her lover's ear
In the secret tongue of desire.

She escalates the cascading syllables
'Till stoked crescendo's peak,
Then hints in more earthly tones
"Fear me..."
But the heart is to potent a percussion
To be outdone by whisper.

Delve

I don't know
What the meter is
Or what of rhyme.
Following the beat of my mind
To where it will me.
Danger lies down this way—
Down the way of impulse.
But what of it?
I delve deeply,
Subconscious know
What lay buried,
Let me find it
To show you.

Devouring the Sun

Dream the demon's corroding dream
And find within a twisting soul.
Diabolic distortions make it seem—
Heart little more than a devouring hole,
Collapsing under intensity grown dim,
All in praise of a hedonist's hymn.

Doppelganger

Every man stands apart
From the shadow that keeps him;
Secure that virtue vanquish vice,
And darkness plot no invasion
Of the realm of lights reign.

In the day the darkling binds
To the heels of his chosen prey.
Little mischief comes from fiend restrained,
But then comes the devouring night
When rogues are known to wander.

Where does the shadow lie
When no light is there to mark him?
He's off to plot a mans demise,
And seal the fate of foul design,
In the bottom of a bottle.

A touch of destiny
Cascades through
The hidden compartments
Of the soul.
Chaos commands
The forces we set in motion
Can only be traced to origin—
never conclusion.
For to study the state
To secure a past explained
Sets a destination
Mysterious.

Etching the Soul

Curiosity chase the busy pen
Down the line of its descent
To find what vision present
The soul a mirror reflecting true—
The love and hate within you.

Grasping the Wind

If you would love the wind–
You can never bottle it.
For you would change the nature
Of that which you would have,
And by its confinement
It is broken.

Gravity

A strong compulsion
To self loathing,
Shared,
Though binding
In orbits of dysfunction–
Possess treacherous expanse
That lies between lovers.

Insomniac

Dark visions lie with me
When sleeps comfort eludes.
They kiss, and cuddle,
And stroke, and strike,
Lull me with whispers
And fill me with fright.

Isolation Chamber

Wish me expressive of all of my pain?
Break me of a will thus constrained-
By a darkness vying for eternal domain,
For all without by all that's contained.

Jacob's Ladder

Scribble a syllable
In vain attempt
To capture a banshee
Screeching in the bad lands.
Like angels on ladders-
Fleeing only to return
A teasing inspiration.

Knocking

Demons, demons everywhere-
How they like to sit and stare.
Come with me and you will find-
The fractured nature of their mind
Is governed not when your alone,
Nor by the will of blood and bone.
Demons, demons knocking on the window
Will you let them in?

Luna's Longing

The lines must break upon the shore
As a lover intent on rhythms remembered,
Consumed by all that's come before–
Yearning the phantom's caress
Renew its devotion
Concealed in the crashing mist.

Mirror's Edge

We bleed to feel our composition,
To show our enemy
A slash of the familiar
In this corporal breaking tide—
Hoping as we lounge among them broken
They no longer see distinction
Between us.

Musing Destiny

A woman rushed the night's embrace
Forsaking the confines of a home not her own—
Urgency compels her, she must know,
If a heart is her's to have,
Or merely borrowed,
For a time too short
To sustain a beat.

She descends the shadowed steps
Of her frantic mind.
Fumbling for coin, she panics;
Charon demands advance,
For no bargain can be made without.
Wind flees her desperation
As she folds into the ground.

Spasms shoot her core,
And reason nearly evades
Through frosted breath of despair;
But as hand clenched,
It felt the resistance it craved,
And eased the payment
Into a devouring grip.

Her back arched in a last revolt
As she pored herself in maelstrom
Into the patient embrace
Of a seat never intent on comfort,
And earned an amused smirk,
For her troubles,
Off the face of her conductor.

Her tears spin as a dervish
Confronted by obsidian waters
Praying that the pounding maintain
Its pulsing comfort—
That passion can maintain
Its meter unfaltering
Through this unfamiliar dance.

Her step demands the ground
Of the spiraled keep.
Her sprint beats the grounding influence
That calls for caution—
Being indifferent
To the painful denial
Of engulfing feeling.

She drags air clawing
In rebellion of her draw
As she supports the faltered entry
Of the feared Moirae.
Question must be posed
By tentative muse restraining
The deluge of her passion.

The maiden naively fair
Spoke only of tender tortures-
Of burning tongues
Shared in earnest,
And raptures of romance
Escaping quivering bodies
Of practicing lovers.

The mother knowing something
Of pulsing embraces
But also something more
Added, "The comfort of compassion
In the grip of despair descending
Is more enduring
A warmth compared."

The crone caressed
Her sheers in mourning,
And spoke of ages past—
Of lover she denied
Out of fear of losing.
She cried these warning words
"He waits!"

Pandora

Abandon to shadows
Haunting the nocturnal
For the feast of souls.
Sacrifice the peace,
For a moment,
The instant before oblivion—
The moment called hope.

Phoenix Rising

I've been dreaming a world
Of gasoline and matches
To thaw the stagnant ice
And bid it rise
To remake the world
In her turmoil
A sharper image
To cut apathy
Out of her heart

Playing Prometheus

Shall my words be remembered or will they fade,
Conducted by wind to the isle of obscurity,
Giving audience to madmen whose gale defeats
Such a modest proposal as hope?
So now I seek the muses nine
For some insight that eludes.
Surely inspiration embodied
Would possess such awareness.
In the solitude of a deep depression,
I found them gathered round,
And asked what words possess
The expanse of eternity.
They spoke with many voices;
They spoke as one.

"Words need not be composed of rhyme-
Nor tell tales of a forgotten time.
They need only eye to see,
And hand to mark their infancy,
So that others might follow more easily."

Playing With Matches

Passion is a rose
Drenched in gasoline
Ignited by the friction
Of thorn breaking skin

Reserved

Play a haunting tune of silence
To a deaf audience
And none shall know it passed

Shiver

I feed on frosted essence
On the way to mirror lake
Bearing the burden of my insulation.

The lake bore no resistance
To my heavy feet,
And ever so briefly
Released me from its grip,
Before smothering me
In its embrace.
Its body shattered
Under the weight of my need,
Granting me audience
With its subdued soul.
There was too heavy an atmosphere
To breach save by shackled howl.

I fled its expansive chambers
And shivered at its door
'Till an attendant saw to my need.
She peeled away the clinging clothes
No longer heeding function,
And added her own flesh
To my exposure
So heat's name be remembered
By breaths shared.

I folded to her calling
As she welcomed me deeper
Into her knowledge of igniting bodies
By friction of meetings.
Static discharge of emotive holes
Cascade through their circuits
'Till spent in the balance.

Memories of these carnal hungers
Reflect in shallow lens
A dimmer view of experience;
But as mad children we pretend
No consequence to our dreaming
Of ever after—
And wake alone.

Tease

The tease,
The tease,
By pouting lips doth summon,
To a meeting yet forthcoming.
For it doth please,
The tease,
To practice her delight.

The Validity of Entropy

Gloom descended upon the lake
As satin sheets upon a new lover
Tentative whether affection be fake
Or do sentiments hold forever.

Mysterious hours by breaths dispatch
In this perturbed sojourn
Through unfamiliar domain to catch
A flame and retain its burn.

Each night be as the last
'Till lovers cease to be sincere.
Powerful as a spell be cast
The failing light draws near.

What Lies Between

There are few things worse then a severed bed
Torn by words composed by a mind consumed
Between heated passions affronted by cold indifference.
For a lover's bed is a hollowed place
Consecrated by a lover's embrace.
More than a compulsion to ease a man's pressure,
Or satisfy a woman's twitch,
A lover's bed is the place
Our truest selves whisper to another;
So be careful never to desecrate
The sacred place with hate.

While You Were Weeping

Sweet children, first you must know—
You did not summon this tempest.
I can not tell, for no one can,
The consequences of this day.

Excuses for this severance
Be offered in excess,
But these causes won't be
What echoes in memory.

I pray you all excused
From so close a place to despair,
But since I lack the power
To influence the sisters of fate,
I offer instead my love
To wrap the wounds of hate.

Witness to a Drowning

The man walks in the night's embrace
Accompanied by the silence
Of half past three
With feet avoidant of ground's commitment,
Yet, each step lingers a moment too long–
Unable to escape completely
From the groping ground.

She had stepped
To that sliding wall of glass
With a forty-five to her face
And asked if he still loved her.
Without waiting for an answer,
She squeezed,
To be with him forever–
If not in love then horror.

The edges of this memory blur
With a last prayer to the bottle
As the grass bends him to its longing,
And soothes him with its sigh
'Till darkness dreams of him.
In waking shadow witnessed
A girl of seven summers
Crouch so man might hear
A curious whisper.

"Why you trying to drown your sorrows?
Don't you know they just float?"

Xibalba

My eyes opened to a sky obsidian
Where the stars raged
To hold back the reigning oblivion.
A fearsome batted waged
Over a soul thus constrained-
By inaction,
By doubt,
By fear.
The desperate hour draws near;
Lest there be in this eternity
Will to bind the fleeing debris,
Cast to darkness,
The shattered key,
To ignite a new furnace.

www.ingramcontent.com/pod-product-compliance
Lightning Source LLC
Chambersburg PA
CBHW031335040426
42443CB00005B/358